GRADE 01

THEORY OF MUSIC PAST PAPERS

May 2018 Grade 1
(A and B papers)

Model answers available online at
trinitycollege.com/pastpapers

Theory of Music Grade 1
May 2018

Your full name (as on appointment form). Please use BLOCK CAPITALS.

_____

Your signature

_____

Registration number

_____

Centre

_____

Instructions to Candidates

1. The time allowed for answering this paper is **two (2) hours**.
2. Fill in your name and the registration number printed on your appointment form in the appropriate spaces on this paper, and on any other sheets that you use.
3. **Do not open this paper until you are told to do so.**
4. This paper contains **six (6) sections** and you should answer all of them.
5. Read each question carefully before answering it. Your answers must be written legibly in the spaces provided.
6. You are reminded that you are bound by the regulations for written exams displayed at the exam centre and listed on page 4 of the current edition of the written exams syllabus. In particular, you are reminded that you are not allowed to bring books, music or papers into the exam room. Bags must be left at the back of the room under the supervision of the invigilator.
7. If you leave the exam room you will not be allowed to return.

Examiner's use only:

1 (20)	
2 (20)	
3 (15)	
4 (15)	
5 (10)	
6 (20)	
Total	

(A-01)

May 2018 (A) Grade 1

Section 1 (20 marks)

Boxes for examiner use only

Put a tick (✓) in the box next to the correct answer.

Example

Name this note:

A ☐   D ☐   C ☑

This shows that you think **C** is the correct answer.

1.1 Name this note:

D ☐   B ☐   C ☐

1.2 Name this note:

F ☐   D ☐   A ☐

1.3 Name the notes to find the hidden word:

ACE ☐   BEG ☐   CAB ☐

1.4 How many quavers are there in a minim?   2 ☐   3 ☐   4 ☐

1.5 Add the total number of crotchet beats in these note values and rest:

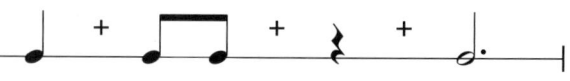

=   5 ☐   6 ☐   7 ☐

May 2018 (A)   Grade 1

Put a tick (✓) in the box next to the correct answer.

Boxes for examiner's use only

1.6   Which rest matches the length of this note value?

1.7   Which is the correct time signature?

1.8   To return the last note to the pitch of the first note, which accidental would you put just before it?

1.9   Which pair of notes has a distance of a semitone between them?

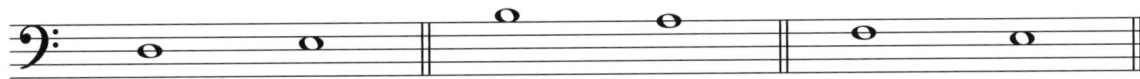

D and E ☐   B and A ☐   F and E ☐

1.10 Which note is the tonic in the key of F major?   C ☐   F ☐   G ☐

1.11 Here is a scale of C major. Where are the semitones?

1   2   3   4   5   6   7   8(1)

Between the 1st & 2nd and 5th & 6th degrees ☐
Between the 4th & 5th and 6th & 7th degrees ☐
Between the 3rd & 4th and 7th & 8th degrees ☐

1.12 How many crotchet beats are in this rest?

2 ☐   4 ☐   1 ☐

May 2018 (A) Grade 1

Put a tick (✓) in the box next to the correct answer.

1.13 Which chord symbol fits above this tonic triad?

F ☐   C ☐   G ☐

1.14 Name this interval:

unison ☐   3rd ☐   2nd ☐

1.15 Name this interval:

5th ☐   4th ☐   3rd ☐

1.16 Which notes would you find in the tonic triad in the key of G major?

GBG ☐
GAB ☐
GBD ☐

1.17 Which note needs to be added to make a tonic triad in the key of C major?

E ☐   C ☐   F ☐

1.18 What does **Moderato** mean?

Fast ☐
At a walking pace ☐
At a moderate pace ☐

1.19 What does the sign > mean?

Play with an accent ☐
Very loud ☐
Play smoothly ☐

1.20 An articulation mark tells a player:

how loudly or softly to play ☐
how to play the notes ☐
what speed to play the music ☐

May 2018 (A) Grade 1

Section 2 (20 marks)

2.1 Write a one-octave G major scale in semibreves, going up. Use the correct key signature and mark the semitones with a bracket (∧ or ∨) and an **S** for semitone.

2.2 Write a one-octave arpeggio of F major in semibreves, going down then up. Add the correct key signature.

Section 3 (15 marks)

3.1 Circle five different mistakes in the following music, then write it out correctly.

(Please turn over for section 4)

May 2018 (A)   Grade 1

Section 4 (15 marks)

4.1   Answer the following rhythm:

Section 5 (10 marks)

5.1   Here is an ostinato. Write two more repeats of the pattern.

May 2018 (A)   Grade 1

Section 6 (20 marks)

Look at the following piece and answer the questions below.

6.1   In which major key is this piece? _____

6.2   Write a Roman numeral below the last note of this piece to show that the tonic triad should accompany it.

6.3   How many crotchet beats are there in each bar? _____

6.4   Put a bracket (⌐¬) above a one-octave scale in the key of this piece.

6.5   What does **Allegro** mean? _____

6.6   Name the interval between the two notes marked with asterisks (*) in bar 2. _____

6.7   How many times does the rhythm ♩ ♫ ♩ appear? _____

6.8   Write the highest and lowest notes in this piece as semibreves.

6.9   What does **rit.** mean? _____

6.10   Should the notes in bar 2 be played *legato* or *staccato*? _____

Theory of Music Grade 1
May 2018

Your full name (as on appointment form). Please use BLOCK CAPITALS.

Your signature

Registration number

Centre

Instructions to Candidates

1. The time allowed for answering this paper is **two (2) hours**.
2. Fill in your name and the registration number printed on your appointment form in the appropriate spaces on this paper, and on any other sheets that you use.
3. **Do not open this paper until you are told to do so.**
4. This paper contains **six (6) sections** and you should answer all of them.
5. Read each question carefully before answering it. Your answers must be written legibly in the spaces provided.
6. You are reminded that you are bound by the regulations for written exams displayed at the exam centre and listed on page 4 of the current edition of the written exams syllabus. In particular, you are reminded that you are not allowed to bring books, music or papers into the exam room. Bags must be left at the back of the room under the supervision of the invigilator.
7. If you leave the exam room you will not be allowed to return.

Examiner's use only:

1 (20)	
2 (20)	
3 (15)	
4 (15)	
5 (10)	
6 (20)	
Total	

(B-01)

May 2018 (B)   Grade 1

Section 1 (20 marks)

Boxes for examiner's use only

Put a tick (✓) in the box next to the correct answer.

Example

Name this note:

A ☐   D ☐   C ☑

This shows that you think **C** is the correct answer.

1.1 Name this note:

D sharp ☐   F sharp ☐   D natural ☐   ☐

1.2 Name this note:

G ☐   B ☐   F ☐   ☐

1.3 Name the notes to find the hidden word:

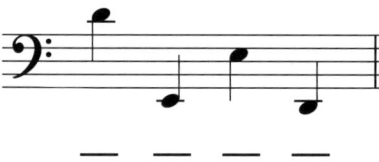
_ _ _ _

BEAD ☐   DEAF ☐   DEED ☐   ☐

1.4 How many crotchet beats are there in a minim?   2 ☐   3 ☐   4 ☐   ☐

1.5 Add the total number of crotchet beats in these note values and rest:

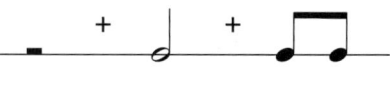

=   7 ☐   6 ☐   5 ☐   ☐

2

May 2018 (B) Grade 1

Put a tick (✓) in the box next to the correct answer.

Boxes for examiner's use only

1.6   Which rest matches the length of this note value?

1.7   Which is the correct time signature?

1.8   To return the last note to the pitch of the first note, which accidental would you put just before it?

 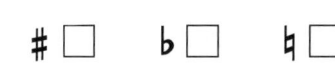

1.9   Which pair of notes has a distance of a semitone between them?

G and A ☐   A and B ☐   B and C ☐

1.10 Which note is **doh** in the key of F major?   C ☐   F ☐   G ☐

1.11 Here is the scale of C major. Where are the semitones?

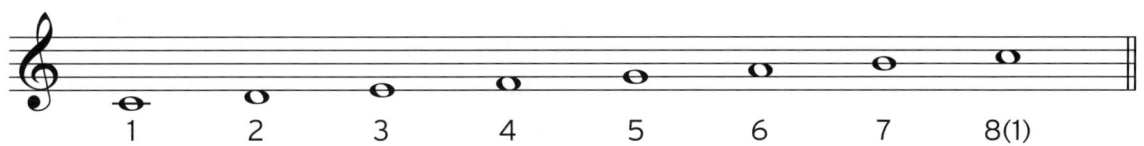

Between the 1st & 2nd and 3rd & 4th degrees ☐
Between the 3rd & 4th and 6th & 7th degrees ☐
Between the 3rd & 4th and 7th & 8th degrees ☐

May 2018 (B) Grade 1

Put a tick (✓) in the box next to the correct answer.

Boxes for examiner's use only

1.12 Which major key has the following key signature?

G major ☐   F major ☐   C major ☐

1.13 Which chord symbol fits above this tonic triad?

C ☐   F ☐   G ☐

1.14 Which note needs to be added to make a tonic triad in the key of F major?

F ☐   A ☐   B flat ☐

1.15 Name this interval:

3rd ☐   4th ☐   5th ☐

1.16 Name this interval:

unison ☐   2nd ☐   octave ☐

1.17 A dot after a note means:

that the note should be played staccato ☐
that the note should be played smoothly ☐
that half its value is added to its length ☐

1.18 What does ⟨ mean?

Getting gradually louder ☐
Getting gradually softer ☐
Play with an accent ☐

May 2018 (B) — Grade 1

1.19 The following is:

- a scale going down ☐
- an arpeggio going up ☐
- an arpeggio going down ☐

1.20 **Andante** means:

- fast ☐
- at a walking pace ☐
- at a moderate pace ☐

Section 2 (20 marks)

2.1 Write a one-octave F major scale in semibreves, going up. Use the correct key signature and mark the semitones with a bracket (∧ or ∨) and an **S** for semitone.

2.2 Write a one-octave arpeggio of G major in semibreves, going up then down. Use a key signature.

Section 3 (15 marks)

3.1 Circle five different mistakes in the following music, then write it out correctly.

Allegro

May 2018 (B)   Grade 1

Section 4 (15 marks)

Boxes for examiner's use only

4.1   Answer the following rhythm:

Section 5 (10 marks)

5.1   Here is an ostinato. Write two more repeats of the pattern.

May 2018 (B) Grade 1

Section 6 (20 marks)

Look at the following piece and answer the questions below.

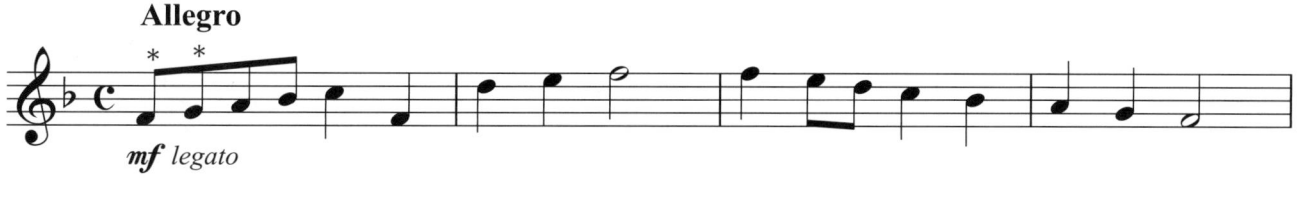

6.1 In which major key is this piece? _____

6.2 Should this piece be played smoothly or detached? _____

6.3 How many crotchet beats are there in each bar? _____

6.4 Put a bracket (⌐¬) above the place where there is a one-octave scale in the key of this piece.

6.5 In which bar is the rhythm the same as bar 1? _____

6.6 Name the interval between the two notes marked with asterisks (*) in bar 1.

_____

6.7 **Doh** is written in two registers in this piece. Put a box (☐) around an example of a high and a low **doh**.

6.8 For how many crotchet beats does the rest in bar 8 last? _____

6.9 What does **Allegro** mean? _____

6.10 What is the loudest dynamic in this piece? _____